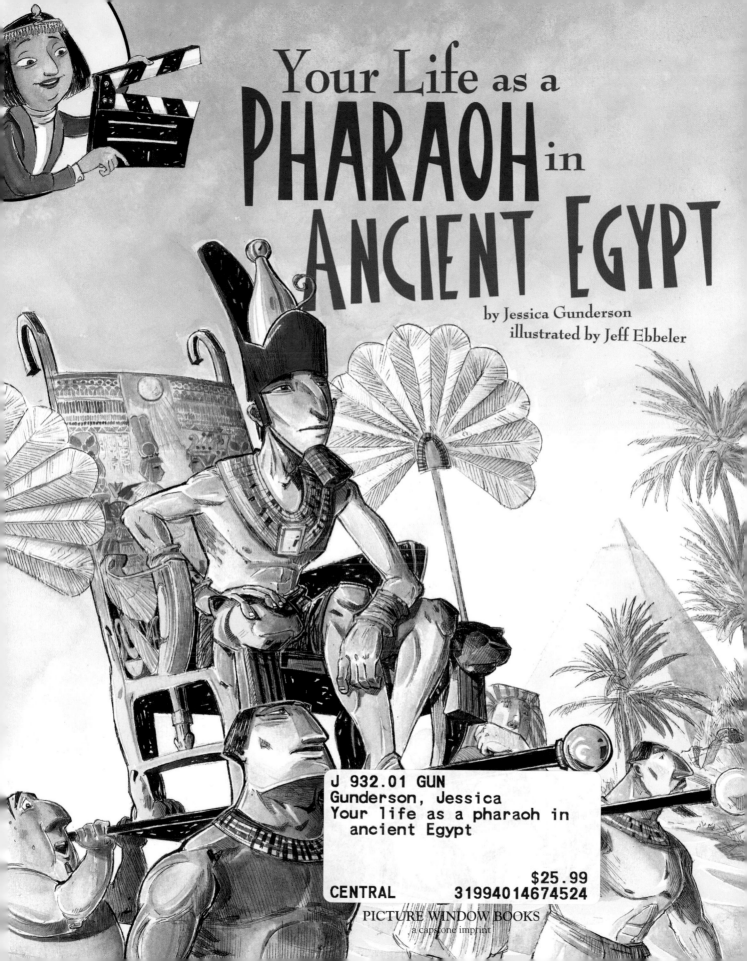

Your Life as a PHARAOH in ANCIENT EGYPT

by Jessica Gunderson

illustrated by Jeff Ebbeler

PICTURE WINDOW BOOKS
a capstone imprint

Thanks to our advisers for their expertise, research, and advice:

Colleen Manassa, PhD
William K. and Marilyn M. Simpson Associate Professor of Egyptology
Department of Near Eastern Languages and Civilizations
Yale University

Terry Flaherty, PhD
Professor of English
Minnesota State University, Mankato

Editor: Jill Kalz
Designer: Ashlee Suker
Art Director: Nathan Gassman
Production Specialist: Kathy McColley
The illustrations in this book were created with ink and acrylic paint.

Picture Window Books
1710 Roe Crest Drive
North Mankato, MN 56003
www.capstonepub.com

Library of Congress Cataloging-in-Publication Data
Gunderson, Jessica.
  Your life as a pharaoh in ancient Egypt / by Jessica Gunderson ;
illustrated by Jeff Ebbeler.
       p. cm. — (The way it was)
  Includes index.
Summary: "Explains what daily life was like for a pharaoh in the Old Kingdom of ancient
Egypt by giving the reader the lead in the school play "Life in Ancient Egypt"—Provided
by publisher.
  ISBN 978-1-4048-7371-1 (library binding)
  ISBN 978-1-4048-7744-3 (paperback)
  ISBN 978-1-4048-7999-7 (ebook PDF)
  1. Pharaohs—Juvenile literature. 2. Egypt—Kings and
rulers—Juvenile literature. 3. Egypt—Civilization—To 332
B.C.—Juvenile literature. I. Ebbeler, Jeffrey, ill. II. Title.
  DT83.G86 2013
  932'.01—dc23   2011050239

Printed in the United States of America in North Mankato, Minnesota.
042012   006682CGF12

YOUR ROLE

Congratulations! You'll be playing the role of Pharaoh Nebibi in our play "Your Life as a Pharaoh in Ancient Egypt." The year is 2401 BC. As pharaoh you'll travel in style. You'll build your own pyramid (or, rather, command others to build it for you). And you may even uncover a mummy along the way.

Ready?

Prepare to rule!

Your Life as a
Pharaoh in Ancient Egypt

Gods Among Us

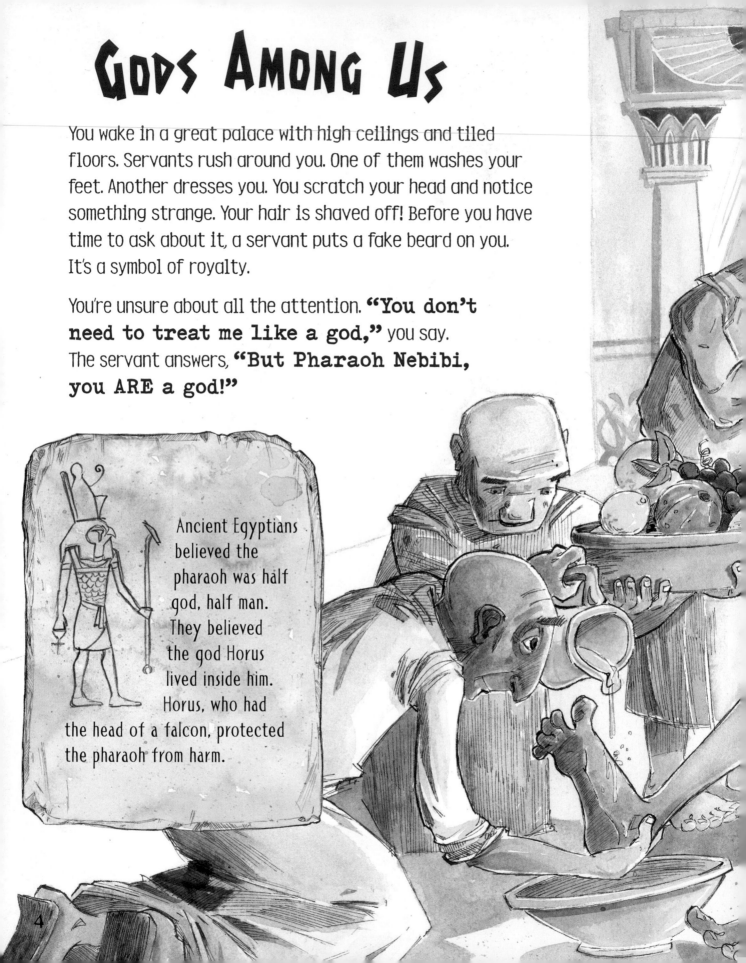

You wake in a great palace with high ceilings and tiled floors. Servants rush around you. One of them washes your feet. Another dresses you. You scratch your head and notice something strange. Your hair is shaved off! Before you have time to ask about it, a servant puts a fake beard on you. It's a symbol of royalty.

You're unsure about all the attention. **"You don't need to treat me like a god,"** you say. The servant answers, **"But Pharaoh Nebibi, you ARE a god!"**

Ancient Egyptians believed the pharaoh was half god, half man. They believed the god Horus lived inside him. Horus, who had the head of a falcon, protected the pharaoh from harm.

5

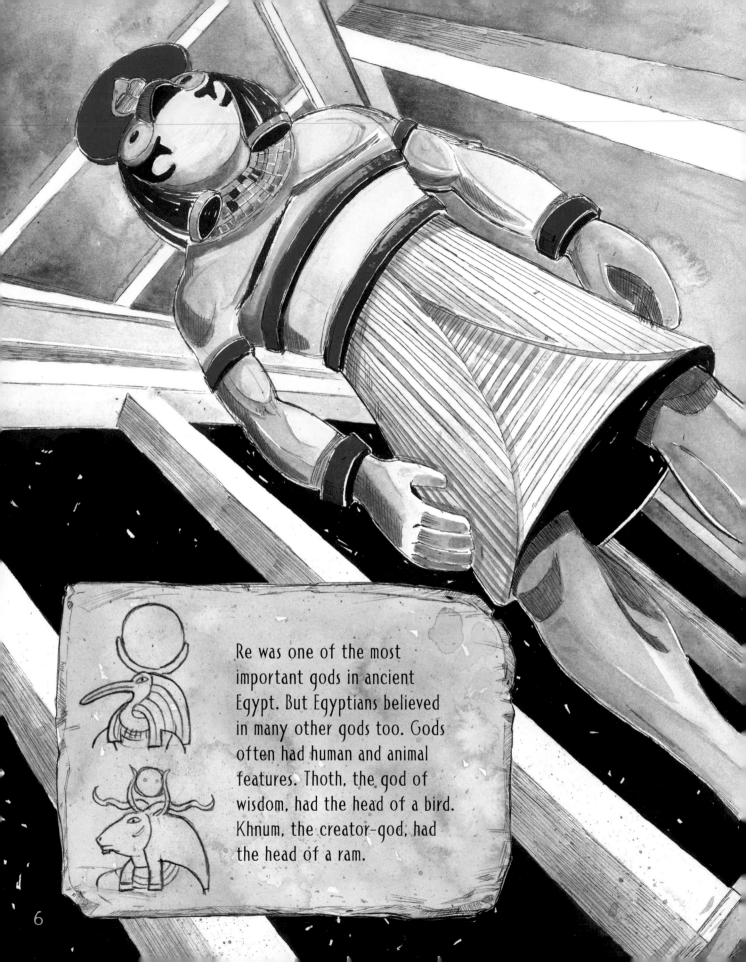

Re was one of the most important gods in ancient Egypt. But Egyptians believed in many other gods too. Gods often had human and animal features. Thoth, the god of wisdom, had the head of a bird. Khnum, the creator-god, had the head of a ram.

TIME FOR PRAYER

Now that you're dressed, it's time to go to the temple. You and the queen must pray to the god of the sun, Re. In return, Re will keep Egypt safe.

The high priest meets you inside. Tall columns fill the temple's dark halls. In the sanctuary you bow in front of Re's statue. **"What must I do to please you, Re?"** you ask the statue. Silence. After a few moments, the high priest answers, **"He says you must build a temple for him near your pyramid."**

A Short Life

Manu, your closest advisor, is waiting for you. You tell him of Re's wishes. Manu looks worried. **"Hopefully your pyramid will be done soon,"** he says. **"It needs to be finished before you die."** You frown. You're not old! Why should you think about death now? But Manu knows best, so you nod and say, **"We should go check on it."**

Break a leg, Nebibi! Egyptian doctors were very good at setting broken bones. They were famous throughout the ancient world for their *medical skills*. However, despite this fact, most ancient Egyptians didn't live more than 40 years.

Pyramids weren't just for looks. Pharaohs and other royalty were buried deep inside the pyramids, along with their treasures. Building a pyramid took hundreds of workers about 20 years to complete. Work on a pharaoh's pyramid may have begun the day he took the throne.

9

MEETING WITH MERCHANTS

Before you can visit the pyramid, you must return to the palace for meetings. A scribe writes down everything you say on a sheet of papyrus.

Merchants from the distant land of Syria approach. They bow until their noses hit the floor. **"Great Pharaoh, we'd like to trade silver for gold and incense,"** they say. You ask, **"Do you have any gifts for me?"** One of the merchants nods and holds out a silver drinking cup.

Can you figure out what the scribe is writing? Ancient Egyptians developed one of the oldest forms of writing, called hieroglyphs. Back then, not many people knew how to read or write, so the scribe was an important person.

Trade was a necessary part of ancient Egyptian life. Coins and paper money had not been invented yet, so merchants traded items. Often they gave gifts to the pharaoh.

The Nile River, the longest river in the world, was the lifeline of ancient Egypt. Merchants had to travel the Nile to reach other lands. Egypt made a lot of money from trading with merchants and other river travelers.

Mediterranean Sea

Red Sea

Nile River

DOWN BY THE RIVER

Whew! You're tired after the meetings. But you still need to travel to your pyramid. At least you don't have to walk, like other people do. Servants carry you in a royal chair to the Nile River.

The Nile buzzes with activity. Fishing boats glide past. Farmers collect water to irrigate their fields. A falcon soars overhead, and you smile. You know that the god Horus is watching over you.

THE TAX MAN

When you reach the Nile, all activity stops. Everyone bows. One farmer is kneeling near a Nilometer. The stone column measures how high the river is. **"Will you ask the god Hapy to give us a large flood this year?"** the farmer asks you. You nod. **"As long as you pay your taxes,"** you say.

You heard right, Nebibi. Your people want a big flood! Floods were good, not bad. Flooding brought water to crops planted near the river.

Taxes in Egypt were paid in a number of ways. Farmers gave the pharaoh some of their crops. Fishermen and hunters gave him fish and game. Craftsmen, such as woodworkers and stonecutters, planned the pharaoh's buildings. Other Egyptians paid their taxes through labor.

15

PYRAMID IN THE DESERT

The royal boat carries you upriver and drops you off. After some distance you see your pyramid rising from the sand. It's covered with tiny specks—hundreds of men moving heavy stone blocks. Some are paid craftsmen, but most are citizens. They're working to pay their taxes. You can't help but feel a little sorry for them. All this work just for your tomb! But you are the pharaoh, after all.

A pyramid's four sides evenly faced north, south, east, and west. The angles stood for the sunbeams that lifted the dead pharaoh to the afterlife. Sometimes the point of the pyramid was covered in metal to reflect the sun.

INSIDE THE TOMB

You'd like to see the inside of your pyramid, but it isn't done yet. So you and Manu check out the nearby pyramid of another pharaoh from long ago. Hieroglyphs color the walls of the passageways. They tell stories of the gods.

The main burial chamber is dark. Everything the dead pharaoh needs to guide him to the afterlife is in this tomb. In the center sits a coffin holding the mummy. You look at it and shiver. **"You're not afraid, are you?"** Manu asks. **"Absolutely not!"** you say. **"It's just cold in here."**

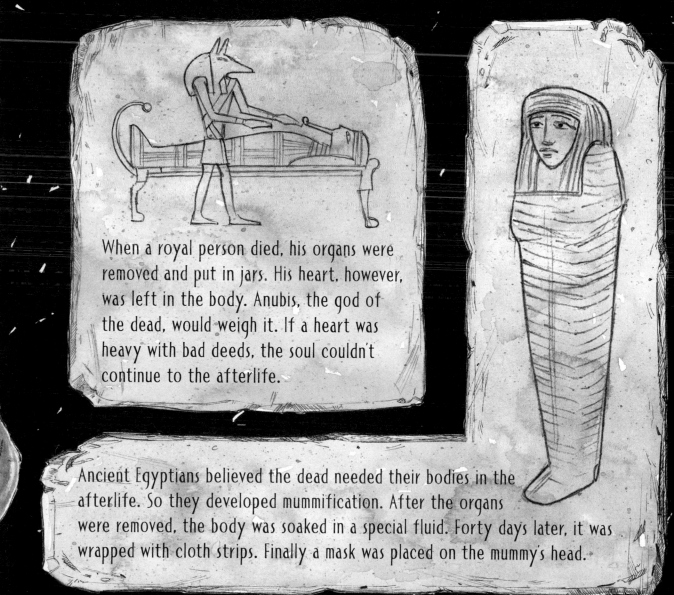

When a royal person died, his organs were removed and put in jars. His heart, however, was left in the body. Anubis, the god of the dead, would weigh it. If a heart was heavy with bad deeds, the soul couldn't continue to the afterlife.

Ancient Egyptians believed the dead needed their bodies in the afterlife. So they developed mummification. After the organs were removed, the body was soaked in a special fluid. Forty days later, it was wrapped with cloth strips. Finally a mask was placed on the mummy's head.

MUMMY'S ALIVE

You hear a sound in the corner. **"Just a rat,"** you tell yourself. But when the rat moves, its shadow grows bigger and bigger. It looms over you. It's no rat! **"MUMMY!"** you cry, grabbing Manu's arm. **"No. Thief!"** he yells. He shakes you off and runs after the figure. By the time you stumble out of the pyramid, the guards have caught the robber. They drag him back to you. You will decide his punishment.

Ancient Egyptians built a number of tombs for their pharaohs above ground. But below ground lay many grand tombs as well. The Valley of the Kings has 63 underground tombs. Egyptians filled them with objects necessary for a good afterlife, including food, clothing, and treasure.

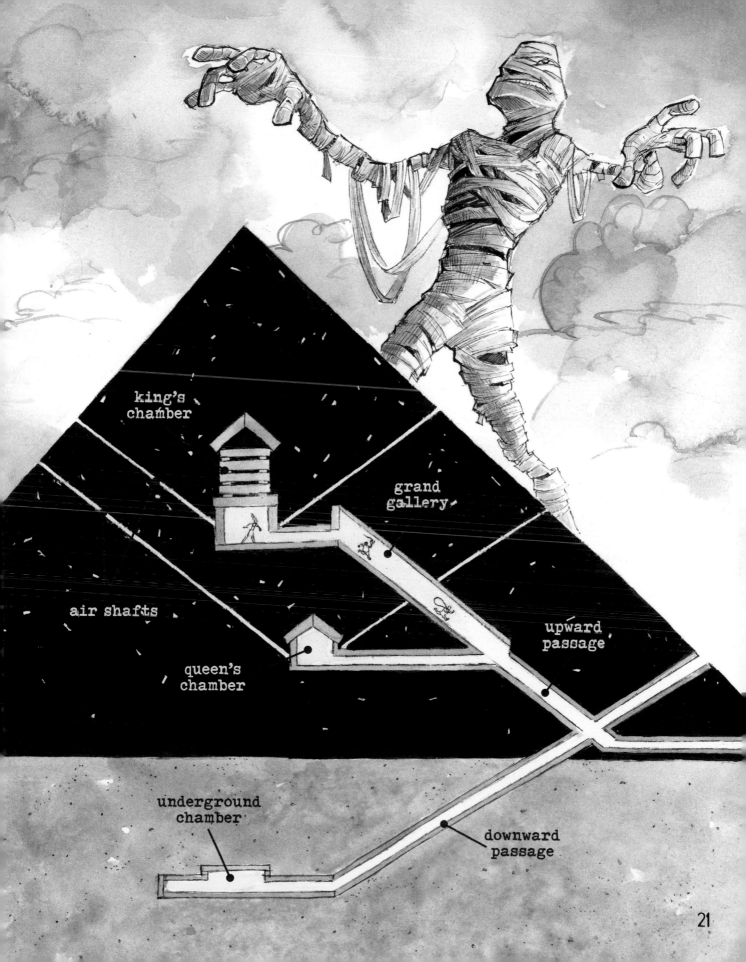

king's
chamber

grand
gallery

air shafts

upward
passage

queen's
chamber

underground
chamber

downward
passage

A Pharaoh's Face Lasts Forever

You head back to your own pyramid. **"I'd like a giant statue right here,"** you say. **"With my face on it."** Manu nods. **"Like the Great Sphinx,"** he says. **"Exactly!"** you say. **"Only mine will be bigger and more magnificent!"** Manu reminds you that it will take many men to build such a statue. And you're invading Nubia tomorrow. You may lose many men in the fight.

You sigh. Manu's right. **"I'd better prepare for battle, then,"** you say. **"But before that, I need a meal. Let's go home. I'm starving!"**

The Great Sphinx of Giza is the largest statue in the world. It has the body of a lion and the head of a man. Many people believe the face is modeled after Pharaoh Khafre.

23

Queens couldn't truly become pharaohs, but some women did take the throne. Queen Hatshepsut reigned for 15 years. The most famous Egyptian queen was Cleopatra. She ruled from 69 BC to 30 BC. She's sometimes called the "Last Pharaoh of Egypt." The Romans took over Egypt after she died.

Wives?! Yes, you have more than one wife, Nebibi. Pharaohs often had several wives to make sure at least one son was born.

LIFE OF A QUEEN

The servants have a feast ready for you. You sit next to your wives and children. Your first wife, the queen, is at your side. You gobble up a leg of lamb, figs, vegetables, and a loaf of bread. **"Tomorrow I will fight the Nubians,"** you tell the queen. She nods. **"Don't worry about the palace,"** she says. **"I will take care of everything here."**

WAR!

You travel south for many days to the land of Nubia.
The battle has already begun. Spears and arrows fly.
As soon as your army sees you, they cheer. They find
renewed strength and fight harder. You draw your bow
and march bravely into battle to join them.

TO BE A KID

Weeks later the battle is won. And now all the riches of Nubia are yours! You're tired when you return to the palace. You just want to go to bed. But your oldest son asks you to play a game of Senet. It's a lot like backgammon. He quickly beats you. **"You'll make a good pharaoh someday,"** you tell him. **"Now off to bed. School tomorrow!"**

Your servants massage your feet and prepare your bed. You lie down, looking at the gold and jewels around you. **"It's good to be pharaoh,"** you say before falling asleep.

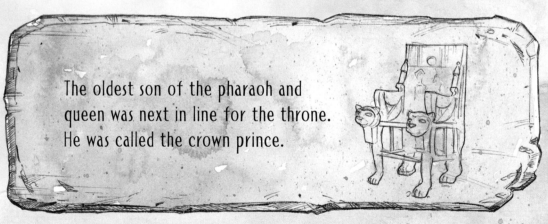

The oldest son of the pharaoh and queen was next in line for the throne. He was called the crown prince.

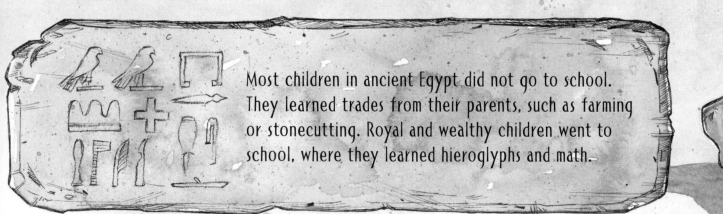

Most children in ancient Egypt did not go to school. They learned trades from their parents, such as farming or stonecutting. Royal and wealthy children went to school, where they learned hieroglyphs and math.

FINALE

Take a bow, Pharaoh Nebibi! What? You don't know how? You're so used to people bowing to YOU? Well, I hate to tell you, but it's time to leave the pyramids and the mummies and go back to being a regular kid.

Wait a second ... the audience is bowing to you! They must believe you really WERE a pharaoh. **Nice job!**

GLOSSARY

afterlife—the life that some people believe begins when a person dies

chamber—a room in a building

hieroglyph—a picture or symbol used in the ancient Egyptian system of writing

incense—a material that produces a pleasing smell when burned

irrigate—to supply water for crops using channels or pipes

merchant—a person who buys and sells goods for profit

Nubia—an ancient country made up of parts of present-day Egypt and Sudan

papyrus—paper made from the stems of papyrus, a tall, reedy water plant

pharaoh—a king of ancient Egypt

sanctuary—a place of prayer

scribe—a writer in ancient Egypt trained to read and write hieroglyphs

tomb—a grave, room, or building that holds a dead body

INDEX

MORE BOOKS TO READ

Deady, Kathleen W. *Ancient Egypt: Beyond the Pyramids.* Great Civilizations. Mankato, Minn.: Capstone Press, 2012.

Jestice, Phyllis G. *Ancient Egyptian Warfare.* Ancient Warfare. Pleasantville, N.Y.: GS Learning Library, 2010.

Steele, Philip. *Ancient Egypt.* Passport to the Past. New York: Rosen Pub., 2009.

INTERNET SITES

FactHound offers a safe, fun way to find Internet sites related to this book. All of the sites on FactHound have been researched by our staff.

Here's all you do:

Visit *www.facthound.com*

Type in this code: 9781404873711

Super-cool stuff!

Check out projects, games and lots more at
www.capstonekids.com

LOOK FOR ALL THE BOOKS IN THE SERIES:

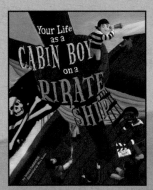

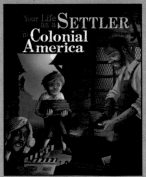